Vetiver

Vetiver

JOËL DES ROSIERS

TRANSLATED BY

HUGH HAZELTON

Signature
EDITIONS

Cover design by Doowah Design.

We acknowledge the support of The Canada Council for the Arts and the Manitoba Arts Council for our publishing program.

Printed and bound in Canada by Marquis Book Printing.

Library and Archives Canada Cataloguing in Publication

Des Rosiers, Joël, 1951–
[Vétiver. English]
      Vetiver / Joël Des Rosiers ; translated by Hugh Hazelton.
Poems
Translation of: Vétiver
ISBN 1-897109-04-0

          I. Hazelton, Hugh, 1946–   II. Title. III. Title: Vétiver. English.

PS8557.E84235V4713 2005   C841'.54   C2005-906907-4

Signature Editions P.O. Box 206, RPO Corydon, Winnipeg, Manitoba, R3M 3S7

for my mother

and my uncles
who opened my eyes
to the beauty
of alchemy

Contents

The grass is defined
By its ways

— François Rabelais

...on the arms of women of other races and there's a taste of vetiver in the underarm perfume of hovering night...

The sea breeze lies over the keys.

— Saint-John Perse

Vettiveru: essential syllables whose exact utterance exhales a light and subtle spirit. The term *vetiver* comes from the Tamil name of the plant whose fragrant roots take on the colour of carnal charity.

I

Cayes

hands precede us
welcome us into the world
shamans' hands midwives' hands
the obstetrician's hands cradle when the moment comes
to fall from the woman's womb that we leave in tears
my share of the legacy was my father's hands
who himself inherited those of his mother Amanthe
whose beauty was mythical
Amanthe died a sudden death
on February 23 1911 at eleven in the morning people yelled fire
it was Thursday the day of wrongs the city was in flames
wind-borne soot enveloped the house
by four in the afternoon the work of ruin had been accomplished
people thought it was an act of vengeance against the hated
Assyrian merchants
or else the wrath of God

my father's father Dieudonné wrote up the manuscript
several thousand pages it took four virgin arms
to carry it after Amanthe's funeral
he suffered from insanity and put on his white alpaca suit
in his lover's grief he lay down like a tutor
calmed by love and uttering the word ecstasy he died
on the day of his fifty-second birthday in the restrained light
of December Dieudonné died of Amanthe

how is it that with hands there's always at least two
we were jubilant at the way our inheritance grew
spending it like something that belonged to another
a God-given thing in which writing takes the form of a stela
grandiose cenotaph of several million signs
under the gentle afternoon sun his hands joined over the male branch
my father returned to the cemetery like a stranger
three sisters followed him two brothers went before him
the real memory of my father isn't the empty house
or the rocking chairs moving back and forth by themselves
on the veranda
it's the smell of black ink the writing that thunders beneath the ashes
his childish tears collapsing under the weight of the manuscript
he feared his father's wrath he became a typographer

long before my birth into the hands of the obstetrician
who sliced my fingers with a slip of his scalpel
the city was called Cayes
the name the Taino Indians gave
to the reefs of madrepore coral
spread out like five fingers of a hand around the entrance to the harbour
in 1527 a galleon from Aquino was ripped open there
Cayos amphibious places fertile with sea bream and moray eels
sacred rocks looking out to sea
the most moving image of the smallest and most fragile island
fields bounded beautiful lies on the surface of the sea
unstable body somewhere between liquid solid and gas
key is a word that hesitates a word that floats in the light
a transparency a resonance of air more of a light-word
or else the island on which the word on which Dieudonnés' love
was shipwrecked
Cayes is a word that can sink

on October 26 1951 the first caesarian
in the city's history took place no one got any sleep
will my daughter survive
my mother's father asked in his slow magistrate's voice
he repeated the question
and went off beneath the pergola
the Oblate nuns of Mary prayed in the garden
the surgeon's hand opened my mother's womb
from the xiphisternum to the pubis
the tribe exulted in the assumption of blood
the child held the scalpel blade between his hands
at dawn my mother's mother found me bloodless
in the immaculate swaddling clothes smelling of vetiver
O rhizomes your essence punishes the anopheles
and your tannins baptize umbilical wounds
the digital arterioles severed spasmed by ether
reopened during the night a blood clot in the mouth
the child had held the wound to his lips
people thought it was a miracle my mother's father quoted *Praise!*
Ah! the keys, our flat houses the city of Les Cayes
where I was born with wounded hands is still there
at land's end at the tip of the tongue of land
on the peninsula that paradise comes from
at the very tip of the tongue

my father assembled the lower-case letters
he had fine elegant hands overwhelmed he thought
he had inherited a manuscript and a woman's hands
so that those hands so foreign to him had become
the indecent trace of a too lovely beauty
to the pitiful tender point
that to hide them from his own view he found himself fated
to the excruciating torture
of endlessly having to hoist himself up as high as carnal extremities
using the lead letters he wrote
Joël has drowned in blood
he let the letters *o* and *d* of *drowned* fall into their boxes
adding the diaeresis over the *e* as they dropped jingling into place
the death rattle of the diaeresis was like a song lodged since dawn
in *Taïno* or *Caraïbe* the sound of the diaeresis was ineffable
he mused over how the diaeresis made him think of the name *Haïti*
a way of accentuating the trembling vowels
the resonance of the beloved letters *a ï e*

he shivered at having chosen that name that sounded like the cry
of a newborn goat toward limbo
who calls out to us in these times of curfew he asked
his fingers had taken on the colour of lead
the nails discoloured with filings
tiny particles had gotten under
the half-moons he caressed the saturnine moons of his hands
the letters rubbed against his leather apron
pure jewels
announcing the resurrection of tongues
one day he wanted to have a taste of ink in his mouth
he poisoned himself with his own hands
the idea came to him of sending off the manuscript
as he breathed his last beneath the dust of the attic beams
comforting the dead man before he could come back
his soul locked away in the buffet
frightened my father gave up typography

like my father's father I assemble the signs
that's not a fantasy that's not an image
I search I go back to the source I want to know who
bequeathed me these atypical hands you have the hands of my mother
Malebranche like my father's mother's last name
the male branch has rosebushes
I could never have imagined how dear a tribute
I'd have to pay to maternal suffering
to Amanthe's passing
to my mother's frightful scar
to the silence surrounding Dieudonné's manuscript
before finding myself years later
a scalpel in one hand and a pen in the other
an homage to Scherer Adrien who sliced me when I was born
stigmata that I carry like a wedding ring on my left hand
incarnation of a strange ease with my hands
among the entrails I say farewell to once more it wasn't enough at all
I have to add pages to the manuscript of darkness
whose first name I carry hidden beneath the form
of a mysterious tautology Ioél God is God
Yah is Él great and terrible

I went to the meeting of noble men
in the paving of their name spelled out loud
that of the ancestor and his pages that a handwriting overloads
in which simple objects with three points are noted down
funeral amulets
made of clay or seashells planted in the soil of the word
to make manioc grow the inhalers of powder
for nights studded with white-tailed eagles
an entire people standing on ships made from gum trees
Dieudonné had the cult of the peoples of the peninsula those who
beneath the arrogance of winds
their skin red as the seeds of the annatto tree
and the tender pulp of words
savannas keys hurricanes and their conquest of islands
from down in the Orinoco
they spread up to Jamaica pushing other islands
farther out
beyond false Mediterraneans
building dance sites
playgrounds during syzygies
vomiting up their entrails and smoking tobacco

father of my father that I never knew
I carry your living faith in the cult of books
in this winged way the petroglyphs he collected
the amulets tucked away hurriedly under the colonist's sticky gaze
engraved with condors with their heads worn away by the summits
and frightened prey in their greenhouses
he concluded that the first natives had known the Andes
before the coasts of Venezuela that stretch out there in the evening
of his life at the speed of scientific dream which is worth
seeing the river's divided shores
and farther still in the great
gourds the crouching faces of the dead placed along the footpaths
between the arum lilies of the open sea and the eddies of battles
I advance toward the key where I was born
such is the foolhardiness of nostalgia
in the vast blue breach that transfixes the fisherman
but welcomes the unknown desire in your tongue

remembering the faces of men
and their air of drowned bodies in stone
faces full of horror and melancholy traces
from some distant damned time they emerge from the South
their consciences tormented by the silhouettes of breastless women
places of conception covered in ferns and fuschia
that you breathe in wildly as you listen to the song of the bats
the desire to watch at the entrance to evil black caves
the shadow of fowls suspended from the ceiling
the air tainted by their droppings
squatting next to the book moved by a filial instinct he opens it
my father's father having copied the simple lines
retouched the monochrome shadows
a happy life like in the Indian kingdoms
before the Christian rot the unashamed diseases
poetic jousting
along with the dances songs and contempt for death
homage thus rendered
to the red inhabitants of basins and plains
everything is epic their civilization renowned
and I dream of the whiteness of Europe

both of them Amanthe and him cut down in the prime of life
O Virgin Muses all I need every morning
is his bearing of an austere ancestor like in the great days
of ancient times he would speak Latin
the language of not-so-dead mathematics
the foundation of intelligence and grammar was a code of ethics
marching toward a paradise of harmony and music where he followed it
not out of pride but from pure love of the prose of empty water
free or else loved by her alone not even by the six children
that he orphaned within a month to the day along with my small self
who has never even seen a photo aside from the Book
and we also were unhappy in our wonder years about his smile
about his only lover who had charmed the broad brief life
he'd barely bent over the tomb he preferred the creole woman's beauty
to reading authors about the last moments of Rome
O Ammien Marcellin

or reread Augustine the African or else Apuleis's *Florida*
all the fine old humanist booty driven out of memoirs and lexicons
of old Europe abandoned here and there
to the point of no longer feeling
the joy of scholarship taking on the other world in ecstasy
having named their sons Stuart Oswald
the names of Scottish heroes who died for their country
from the bedroom window overlooking the main square
where he put away the speeches on May 18 stretched out in the alpaca
suit he used to wear as he strode across the city
like a black jaguar lithely gliding
his right hand subjugating the guaiacum tree
the male lying in wait for beauty like in his dream
O mulatto woman smoking
cigars his brain inundated with the penumbra of creole happiness
and ever since here they are sure of their triumph after the wedding
at times speaking African Latin with the other Guillermina sisters
Hermance and the youngest who was hunchbacked
beauties appearing fleetingly disappearing
the murmur of death accumulates in his body as
he orders more volumes from Paris
the priest's dogs bark at the shadows of stained glass
gentle beasts you have to knock senseless

the language reappears in the loss the words rise up again in dialect
and jostle the ancient tongues in his heart where Massillon
father of Dieudonné known as Marcius
the name of the slave who defied Caesar
instilled along with the obligatory verses of the *Aeneid*
Phaedra's fables still ringing in his ears
enjoying the music
of reciting
the pure meaning *nunc pede libero pulsanda tellus*
and the dive into Lucretius or Lucan before the free teaching
of Martial or Petronius or even the *Persian Satires*
brought up by women and dead at twenty-eight
preparing his son for the written necessity of language
in the ownerless mouth
we honour those who have left us our great dead
who after their apothecary studies in Bordeaux
would only consciously recite poets who'd turned savage
before the disgusting rabble with the louder throat
could lay their unfinished words in our hearts with the roosters
and drums and the *Remedies for Love* could reign over us
the cherished children of the gods who are soothed with laudanum

O Cayes for all the lands and all the races
seven hundred and two houses in the island's marshes
teeming with crocodiles and your eyes wander over the madrepore coral
that the sky has washed purged of creatures gathered within walls
four thousand five hundred fifty inhabitants
one thousand three hundred whites
three hundred freemen and women three thousand slaves
plus a hundred indolent and rare sailors and soldiers
visiting the battlefields where they go to suffer
it's a beautiful silent city among the vetiver grasses
the historians comment on the victory of the Maroons at Plymouth
Voodoo emerges from the rain forests of the Sudan and finally descends
from its African Olympus to set up camp on the terraces of Macaya
and the Roman madonna flees to the Lower Keys as Audubon's
mistress how many wood pigeons do you have to paint
for the glory of your native town a shadow hangs over your birth
it was time to flee to France
the women in African dresses were advancing
their skin covered with bites

out of despair at death which has foreseen everything
out of despair at the world which is only illusion
out of despair at time which is nothing but dust
the universe is living the mountains the caves
the rivers the sea with its pierced side the souls of men
and beasts that tremble above the great crossroads
the earth is thin between deep waters
a disk floating upon the cosmos of water and stars
a black hole straddles the body of the earth
all memory has flown off on its wings
that have wounded the heart of the world from the beginning
will I see like the shaman the signs traced along the surface of things
there are still hours to go on the journey traced by legend
there are still gestures and I've smoothed out
the stone images with my fingers

our poem is very old moved by the light wind
didn't you believe in bygone times in enjoying things like the crowd
myths included in banality contemplating my grandfather's
ordinary and splendid Book swollen with symbols where he poured out
his own reflections to dull your imagination
what would happen to your race a memory of legends a decrepit
lyricism of religiosities the fall into disjointed rhymes
confused solidarity of everyone ever exploited the epic of vanished
peoples the poetry of children and fields
is it also sought more and more in prose
in the beautiful and strange sonorities left to us by
our predecessors in misfortune give me the atmosphere
of splendour of peoples sacrificed to gold replaced
by others who will be offered up to sugar cane and cotton

subtle elder your urgent and just prose surges up from the ruts
the feigned anguish of antlerless crowds fades away
all in the emblem of the hero dressed in the turtle's
shell that was my dream about the time of the aboriginals
in which I plunge again into the night of humble times
all names fallen like palm branches
the rosebush kid language forbidden so exempt me
from the fulminations insults forgotten deaths it's well
known that they would cut your throat like vanquished enemies
at dawn to the bone tibias and olecranons
left exposed to the elements in great gourds
suspended from the rooftops or else at the height of a poem
your toothed heads emerge to watch us improvise
the text like those recited in temples but in fact
taken from the forebear's Book applied to the nocturnal labour
of his memoirs before he could reread them beneath the leather cover
in a grandiose spectacle turning the pages away from the sacrilege
of descendants like Paultre get some ink
under your nails he tore one off it was so beautiful that he received
the language prize O black widower dying from his lover

after the burial in the pain of love
the Secret returns to the oldest son the impenetrable uncle named Stuart
who made his girl cousins laugh when he imitated jungle sounds
in a grand soundless gesture
he confides the volume to the mahogany sideboard
the eyes outside staring at complete oblivion the rustled silence
of the flight of owlet-moths next to the black shoes and starched
collars is it Duvivier Hall is it Ernest Douyon or
perhaps Louis Marius giving the funeral oration for the man
lying in a white suit that is impeccably becoming
in the December elegance of my father's
father's face drowned in the canal of love under a sheet
of scarlet thread without the help of dances and
chants devouring my face since then I wander through the vanished Book
the staggered rows of pages where the tents of India and the Orient
unfurl imagined by this austere man
right off I catch the scent of vetiver
for rubbing into books and wooden frames

our dead in the earth beneath the huts O our dead
don't die in the islands to come they live
deep within our throats our voice is theirs
it's their bones that quiver in our words
tell this to your sons and your sons to another age
the powerful sadness of love is it that way you
dream of me what have you hidden that isn't lost
the pages written by pinpoint through the night among the phosphenes
slow curves of vocabulary and missives
quench their thirst in the disease's black carnality
leave me now to the happiness that lacerates me
there to live the splendour of late afternoons
my body moulded by tuff shadow writing darkness

the first poets speak to the first peoples
what else have they ever wanted
the streets flow through the night the churches filled
with evil spells and in public places besieged
by crowds constantly wanting to revive the dead man
his misfortune in life transmuted into joy in writing
buried as of tomorrow beneath the couch grass of India
at the moment your tears from nineteen twenty-eight on
flower every year in a green lightning bolt of macaws
the son happy at having such a fine example before his eyes
of a man of letters fermented by death
his hand between the legs of the mulatto woman he loved
love is his silence the music around without a sound
of the tender earth that his ashes face
O childhood that discovers the plain

II

For Vaïna,
The Illustrious Servant

the wind in the treetops made their voices come rushing back
she passionately wanted to be alone
only in secret did she dream of vast empty spaces
empty of those slow bodies empty of voices
when the sun reappeared it was already too late
and the gully in the distance and the sea
through the tops of the mangroves
she could see that light she had wished for so much
she stopped under the cover of a tree
on public benches other women scantily dressed
in bright colours waved to her

daylight had seduced her
she felt thunderstruck
thrown like a foreigner into an unknown city
solitude seemed like a stigmata
indifference scorn rejection succeeded in
craftily splitting open her body
she edged along the wrought-iron gates
in the neighbourhood called Gabion des Indigènes
she didn't care whether the properties protected
by high walls crowned with broken glass were beautiful or not
her hands and forearms moved
like shapeless shadows
wandering down to the park despising the flowers
she felt suffocated with tears that refused to come
she began to cough dragged back into the abyss of her throat

she prayed in a low voice in front of the church
trying to decipher the inscriptions
set into the walls on the chains
and iron rings set into the stones
her hand felt the places where sufferings still surfaced
and kept biting slowly at her ankles
she proclaimed within herself the saintliness of bodies impaled long ago
prayed naively stubbornly for the saints
never to abandon her and to appear
she needed miracles of vetiver of redemption

beneath the nave's yellowing whitewash
other women sang on their knees
and cried out their mortified canticles
in Latin which was unknown to her
as if to dissolve into the poem
to brush against the absolute you had to lose your voice
give up the language of your childhood
to achieve strange epiphanies words fled from her
pagan voices filled her with dread
and wonder while their cries
spurting through the cracks rebounded at the feet of the disintegrating
marble reliquaries
she loved that far-off language

she thought her hair skin blood
were nothing but jumbles of body parts
without any connection between them I'm not me she thought
she was afraid of losing her soul in a bottle
of tafia rum from which there was no escape she thought
that her soul was soaking in foul-tasting water
she thought she was alive among the living
doomed to disgust racked by decay
that she was becoming nothing but a semblance
like the dazzling light that spattered her dress
she began to memorize the mortified canticles by heart
in that ancient language they wanted to massacre
she loved the slope of the sounds

the voices vibrated in her skull
like the hymns of slaves
without knowing anything of that language she strove
to repeat the lament the voices found the path
of the spine planes and nerves
when their resonance at the end of neuraxons
became too exquisite I've become sick from chanting she thought
from the verdicts uttered by the women's lips
she believed that the tones they unearthed
were all meant for her
not one of those women with a half-open throat
would have agreed to reveal the madness of those songs
to save her from further mutilation

there was a smell of mangrove in the air
the fertile silt with its impure stench
where secret passions incubated one afternoon suddenly
the hours dwindled as the sun declined
in the elongating shadows of great trees
it appeared to her that there was no common time
for the two parts of the country the city to which she had migrated
with its crossroads parks grand boulevards
the country outside she'd left behind its slow declination
I'm an alien in my own land she thought
she spoke to the male child of the outside
she'd left in the slow heavy tongue
Dieudonné's grandson whom she was raising
now that she'd become his other mother

she had slept in her sleep
through the hours light dreams
in her sleep she thought she saw jubilant crowds
stirring up clouds of dust with their feet
the throng brandished whole pieces of tongues
on the ends of long poles
bloody shreds that outraged the heavens
she was overcome with terror when she saw this human swell
so close so threatening when it wasn't the fear
of having her hypoglossal nerve torn out
there was no tongue to describe the state of mind she sank into
when she awoke there were only remnants

at the end of the courtyard stood the outbuildings
of a house with lace woodwork
surrounded by a veranda overlooking a rose garden
when her bedroom windows were open
they overlooked a garden filled with aromatic plants
as soon as the sun set the night fell warm
shady on the mat where she lay
often nude beneath the thin calico cotton lifeless voiceless
her memories unfit surfaceless
she recalled things that had never happened to her
memory with no one there
distressed within the infinite repetition of ideas images and feelings
she caressed the red veil with her feet
with the fingers of her left hand
the line where the two small lips met
until a kind of blessed annihilation
she twitched softly

she took great pleasure in seeing a mongoose
scamper off amid the baying of dogs
the sky grew dark and the sea
during those hours that belonged neither to day nor night
she fled along the grey river shore with the body
and soul of the child entrusted to her
she sat down upon the crests of the dunes overlooking the sea
and the sea was without beginning
in the distance was Île-à-Vaches
the salt breath of the wind blew in
far-off sails emerged out of nowhere
and more sails still the sea grew rougher
she held the child close against her warmth
speaking to him in her slow voice like you'd speak to flowers
something in the child was transformed
into stems of roses on the ocean floor

there were three drops of blood on the sand
she came out of her brief ecstasy
the living child was handsome she would have liked
him for her own
in the morning the lady of the house reminded her it was forbidden
she went off and disappeared beneath the archway
voices fell upon her brain
as softly as light
it seemed to her that each tongue shrouded another
she surrendered herself as if to a drug
to the solitude and silence

no one will get out alive from the garden of the senses
she thought
the garden was a primeval forest
the child ran through the vetiver grass
in a strange euphoria
the garden was the theatre of muffled murmurings
the breath of flowers was softer
on the air than in her hand
she felt an irresistible urge to caress
the grass and flowers especially after a light rain
in the shade of the spicy ilang-ilang tree that set the evening aglow
she rubbed the child's lips with the illicit root

the child was in his bed
she had no recollection
she wanted to be discreet
lying on the mat
she strained her ears toward him
catching nothing but his sleeping breath in the darkness
an orange triangle shone faintly
on his Achilles' heel
not a single rustle of sheets
nothing exceptional
the hour though she wasn't sure
of the sun burning off the mists
she was used to dawn

on the bedroom wall
which shadow drew
the diurnal remains of her dream
with such strong lines
no one ever knew where she came from
she turned her kneecaps against the damp clay
the furrowed soil pronounced the name Vaïna
the illustrious servant who hugged me in her arms
and my weak arm grasped her breast
all she was wearing was a camisole
the purple nipple erect

pushing open the black iron gate
the evening mist
a great hope at the edge of the gate
she glanced furtively at the destiny of the child
of miraculous birth
she covered him with white vetiver flowers
a miracle amid the clusters
the child touched the breast of the woman he resurrected
she added the male flower unfolding in racemes
the hedge of grasses
young birds alighted
as if she had carried him nine months
within her perfumed sides

thoughts came numerous
lost their way on the gravel in the garden
the child was growing up
she dressed him in linen several times a day
she never returned to the village where she was born
something irreparable happened
that made her sweat and then feel cold
then the river's vortex swallowed up
the deluge slit the land's throat with its sheep-and-cattle barbed wire
the child had looked out upon the flood's horizon
mud flowed from his mouth
what cry formed on his lips
she heaved him up onto the mahogany dresser
and her desperate prayers seemed powerless
the hermetic waters rose to her waist
the image gave life to a desire for silt
and the red roses of the rosary flowed off toward other seas

in remembrance of the curative herb
because of the substance through which the herb
of that name
heightened its powers in the fire the deep herb
between the servant woman's eyebrows
the herb is not the fire but the denial
of the herb in the end ruled by oblivion
obscure lamp seeded with ants
for the bride of the brambles
lively unexplained lamp of brambles
tenacious in its bed of brambles
rekindled by the servant's dark approach
the perennial oil at the herb's foot

pure instrumentalists the child and servant
their hiding place offered at evening
to quiver with them every day
herbs of my descendants
men of pure lineage
through the vow of the useful herb of light beneath the flies
the herb strengthened the knots of sugar cane
herb of eternity advancing from India
O you who know the meaning and the prey
O you who give thatch and paper

III

Cayenne

no one warned me
fascinated by maps of the world
my eyes open wide over atlases
I thought as a child that Cayenne had been founded
by people from Les Cayes where life begins
where women are called Cayennes
despite the passage of time I rediscovered
the myth of far-off times of childhood
when the airplane flew over the anticyclone of the Azores
through the windows haunted by ozone I could
by a kind of recollection measure
the filthy ocean of the slave trade

I wanted to repopulate the motionless sea
and summon
all those I'd never known
or who had drowned to death
no one ever re-emerged from those burning depths
the phantoms of imagination
which I confused with those of reason
pursued me from the open sea

the light alone revived the beings of remembrance
it seemed to me that my memory lingered
saturated with fatigue and that dazzling brightness
from one shore to the other I travelled over the Atlantic
crossing the polar latitudes in a single night
from Montreal to Paris
and then in one stride the spine of the coiled reptile
that lies in its home on the salt surface
beneath the belly of the craft the space and light
sticking together
the plane flew over the longed-for islands
far-off conditions for a soaring poem

or was it the jet lag that numbed my senses
I saw the blue of the sea
tedious almost useless spectacle fade
and then disappear beneath the muddy rivers bringing down
alluvium from Amazonian jungles all along the coast
at the top of the South American continent
pretending to believe in progress that was abolishing borders
and even less in the speed of the machine that already
in a euphoric roar that sprang from its sides
skirted slow clouds
and touched down on the red earth of French Guiana
while the forest shook itself beyond the edge of the city

I abandoned myself to the dangerous pleasure of rediscovering
the promised land of childhood like breasts
a land kept secret from me
and luckily I didn't know how to escape
as if my memory suddenly unblocked
I recognized it without ever having seen it
the stewardess let out a welcome to *Rochambeau* airport
in a voice that faded away
at the threshold of the senses words it seized me like a torment
O airwoman naked grant my wish

childhood is immortality
the student notebooks recitations
of capitals countries the Bolivian lake
angelic names scrawled on bits of paper
passed around secretly shamelessly and called out during recess
names no one understood but
the long words made us laugh drawing the teacher's
wrathful gaze as he threatened us with his vengeance
in sulfurous notes
he would write next to spelling mistakes
notes we would remember forever
not without a certain tenderness
and that we still recall sir

for *Guillane* or the wretched *Caïenne*
your homework is written in a language
which vainly wishes
to seem like French
and even
your insect-like writing
doesn't authorize you to put to *l*'s in *Guyane*
the teacher didn't as much combat our mistakes
as pass on to us
for future years his passion for the language
and fear of any form that went beyond it

Rochambeau airport glowed pink beneath the circles of light
out of all the lobbies waiting rooms and train station foyers
movie theatres banks or synagogues
operation rooms or libraries my only passion
is for airports their signs reading *Arrivals* and *Departures*
that they display inconsistently each contradicting the other
but that link together the dual profiles of the same life
it was a temple of glass panelled in mahogany
the great glass roof held up by steel beams
blinded the concourse with a virginal glow
after the sleepless nights of flight
day murmured white

and suddenly I raised my eyes to a warning
against yellow fever
I'd forgotten to take precautions
the sign suspended my reveries I saw myself
being bitten by mosquitoes that spat out the virus
in the very first seconds
the jaundice hemorrhaging the black vomit
my body in a prostrate night of delirium
filled with boards covered with red fur floating down wild rivers
I dismissed the image with a soundless gesture
once out the door
the vibration of the warm humid air
calmed me down
alive and not alive I pushed the cart forward
my too true existence on the Equator

at four o'clock that afternoon
as I was thinking of my light-bodied stewardess
a bald black man
addicted to nicotine a bit retiring
a bit silent
more Bambara than West Indian judging by his features
it was the consul general of my island birthplace
his hand covered with the fine dust of the country
he made the usual remarks about the beauty of Creole women
the heat and humidity dwarfed my forgetting the vaccine
against yellow fever because it wasn't really worth worrying
too much about hemagogic mosquitoes
that by the grace of God honoured our blood
some tropical diseases were to be feared

the consul general promised me several realistic and amazing
stories about everyday people from the island
that he would tell me about in detail it was a promise
the luxuriance of the vegetation that seemed like an enormous tussock
from up in the air was half composed
of known species that had taken on a grandiose appearance
when planted on the continent and
half from strange indigenous plants
that I first discovered with fervour
like portents admiring how
huge trees straightened up as we came round
a curve the airport suddenly disappeared

Rochambeau the name rose up from the depths
with a disturbing strangeness
is it our Rochambeau
the consul general burst out laughing it was ours all right
they'd wanted to honour the memory of the most detested general
in the whole War of Independence
the villain of the French expedition to Haiti who took refuge
in Guiana after the fall of the colony
before his death Field Marshal Leclerc Napoleon's brother-in-law
had chosen him as his successor
the most senior major general in his army
Donatien Marie-Joseph de Vimeur Vicount of Rochambeau

he returned to Haiti in February 1802
during the worst period of desolation
when he became commander-in-chief of the French army
he looked on helplessly as the yellow fever epidemic
decimated his troops
killing forty to fifty soldiers a day
Cap-Haïtien and Port-au-Prince were transformed
into hospices for the dying
no choice could have been worse for France
in response to the courage and victories of the rebel soldiers
soulless brutes he called them
Rochambeau applied methods of torture
of unbelievable barbarity
forever staining the history
of every nation
that claimed to be civilized

all the blacks and mulattos that could be arrested
were murdered in the most brutal possible way
gallows were erected everywhere
execution by drowning burning at the stake
the most horrible punishments were carried out on his orders
as he invented a new machine of destruction
victims of both sexes piled up on top of one another
were asphyxiated by sulfur fumes in the holds of ships
Rochambeau had decided to pollute
what he called a *filthy hole* with his monstrosities
which went far beyond those of Pizarro Cortés Bodavilla
the first scourges of the New World
several of the acts of the Nero of Haitian occupation
bear witness to a morbid pleasure verging on madness

he enjoyed giving apocalyptic balls
one night he decided to hold a ball for the mulatto women of the city
everyone danced gaily at midnight the guests were shown
into an adjoining room
where men dressed as priests sang the *Dies irae*
before a row of coffins covered with black sheets
Rochambeau explained coldly
to the despairing women mad with terror
that they had just attended the funeral
of their fathers brothers sons and husbands
under suspicion or imprisoned who had been drowned that evening
in the bay

bringing back a Spanish atrocity of the fifteenth century
the general imported mastiffs from Cuba
trained to hunt escaped slaves and used them
as bloody auxiliaries in his revenge
first the dogs were starved
and then to excite them were fed the still-warm
entrails of the blacks who'd just been executed
during the battle of Petit-Goâve the dogs brought in from Havana
by the Vicount of Noailles had their coats extravagantly coiffed
and were dressed in silks and ribbons
that matched the colours of the aristocrats' furbelows
but when they were were unleashed
on the rebel fighters
they turned on their masters and happily
devoured them in the midnight gloom

we arrived at Cayenne in late afternoon
the city was silent as if it were sleeping
at that hour the inhabitants had disappeared
the sun was setting laying down shadows
and across Place des Palmistes the royal palms erect
like demigods you could see the houses
glowing red
ochre
that day I felt I could praise
the gentleness of provincial cities
in nineteen hundred fifty-six the universe
torn apart between two languages the mahogany furniture
three cats crabs in eggplant and great-aunts
the other Circe a woman of letters of haughty virtue
who loved a certain cousin
a Penelope with a beautiful slightly lilting voice
tirelessly played *Air for African Slaves*
on a black piano

my eyes rested on the coiled balusters of balconies
the wrought iron
following the layout of the streets
the two-story wooden houses
the ground floor encircled by a veranda
bathing the city in a green glow
in the odour of humus
a great liking between places and myself
growing in the air and water along the wharf
I couldn't measure the outlines
nowhere could I have been happier
it gave me the illusion of rediscovering the city
from which I'd been taken when I was young
during the violence against the family women
mulattos fathers uncles sons
and husbands

my memories coalesced at that moment
the city streets unreeled to welcome me
I felt neither nostalgia nor tears
the footprints left by people we've loved
remain unbelievable living unexpressed
Cayenne the imaginary city of my childhood
trembled within me immortal counterfeit
in a sort of limbo
exiled city in a foreign continent
tender figure of loss
seated at the edge of the endlessly threatening jungle

the city of Les Cayes is flat and well laid out
keys threatened by high water and cyclones
resuscitated islands divinities in my imagination
steeped like the air with humidity
they reappeared in the words of uncles
the only city in the colony built on the King's orders
according to the architect's plans
the only city with a central square
the orderly streets where I'd often played
their refinement now tattered
there'd been murders with red lips
an army officer's body at the door of the Club Marabou
the slow elegance of passersby in the city of madrepore coral
below the sea and crying
torn out of the sea like a blueprint
O childhood how could I fail to celebrate

night had fallen thickly over Place des Palmistes
I'd been warned
not to venture there alone
at that hour after midnight the skeletal dogs
the wretches
Brazilian prostitutes Georgetown drug addicts
with shining eyes a whole people of darkness
edging along the walls
poured into the night ready to inspect
as I slept I couldn't sleep
all these threads entangled in my brain
the night watchman looked at me annoyed a little worried
as he watched me walk out the doors of the hotel

a few men still on the square
were playing cards by candlelight
they straightened up as I went by without batting an eyelid
hey man *ka nou fè* beneath the trees of peace
his voice disappeared into the thick shadow
I turned down Avenue Léon-Dumas
Pigments of myself
a belated flash of inspiration made me imagine
giving another name to the place
night doll giving in to every instinct
there was a sudden noise
I took out my notebook to write

she spoke with a certain absence in her gestures
saying she wanted a dedication
and that she'd been spying on me long before I arrived in Cayenne
because she'd found out the names of the writers who'd been invited
and had copied my photograph
as well as the uselessly flattering biographical note
that she got off an Internet site
and that photograph she said the one in which
I wore a bow tie that looked like it had been tied by hand
had inspired her to write letters that she addressed to me
but could never bring herself to send
because her thoughts had gotten away from her and in her opinion
it was horrible
to write only for oneself and not send off the letters
to their recipient and so risk leaving them *without even an echo*

she said she'd gone
to the first book fair ever held in Cayenne
to meet me in person
unlike all those people who press forward
without looking or linger
around the books
alone or with their families
enthusiastic or indifferent silent or garrulous
at times without any other reason than simply to be seen there
she came
herself
for a specific reason
to ask me to dedicate a book
to her

because I was she said according to the biographical notes
she'd attentively read both a doctor and a writer
and my double profession
conferred on me in her eyes an exquisite understanding of people
in other words a knowledge of pain
because I looked at them with one eye on their life
and the other on their death
and adding literature to medicine forced me
to give people back the insidious gift
I had received of their suffering
she said that by delving into that space beyond their bodies and
their souls I revealed to others and especially to her
my immense desire to heal and that this understanding of others
presupposed a fascination with misfortune
that she had no trouble understanding and
that was enough for her to trust me

she said that was the main reason she'd spoken to me
and for the sake of which she asked me to be truthful
that is to write just for her
on a card with a reproduction of a painting by Matisse
which she'd specifically brought with her and now placed upon the table
next to the pile of books a sort of portrait
a dedication that would show her truth light and shadow
she said which I was most certainly capable of drawing out from her
from the first time I set eyes on her
from our very first encounter an immemorial
nameless thing that would set her apart from the people around her
and that I shouldn't avoid her request
and that although she was for me a kind of stranger
this shouldn't provide me with any excuses because
when you really thought about it
what she was asking me for didn't have to be that personal

even though she hadn't yet read a single one of my books
she said that my voice which she'd heard on Radio France International
during the program on visiting writers
had crept into her mind strangely enough not so much
for what it actually contained as for the language that carried it along
and more important than the features of my face
which she had already perfectly memorized
in order to recognize me
she had observed the liberated way I moved on television
my origins gave me away she said as I strolled through
Place des Palmistes but what she'd appreciated most of all was
the mixture of intelligence and humour in the comments I made
on the architecture of creole houses adorned with wrought-iron balconies
when the afternoon light made them seem unreal
she said she'd told herself now here's a writer who finally
doesn't take himself too seriously

she said she had only been in Cayenne for a short time
that she had lived before in the 16th arrondissement in Paris
and that she'd come to French Guiana just for a change
perhaps out of nonconformity or because she was bored
and most probably for some reason still unknown to her
she said that even supposing I had wanted to
I couldn't have avoided her request
I was neither a real writer nor a true doctor
or else if I'd risked embarking on both professions
which seemed so opposed to one another it was because she said
I felt free enough of any double association
sufficiently carried along by my double vocation
to answer this kind of question and because she calculated
on observing my photo that behind a sad smile
I was trying to hide a kind of melancholy
that was concealed in my eyes

she said that on account of my destiny
I led a double life
the risks of which I should accept
including that of granting her wish
and that a true writer (which wasn't necessarily what I was)
had the capacity to sound out souls
to be able to feel like others the excessive love that threatens
the devastation of feelings that don't by rights belong to it
and that it's from this ability
that the writer draws the sense of his existence
and what's more she said if I were a true physician
I wouldn't have the slightest chance of escaping her wish
because she could be ill she could be in pain
she could be in distress even without knowing it
and her desire despite the unusualness of the situation
could correspond perfectly to a symptom
a sign even if she wouldn't dream of expressing it that way
of the upheaval of time
and of her way of living triggered by my presence
she said she'd never felt such desire for a dedication

she said she'd come to French Guiana
after having studied a bit of music and literature
taken some courses in playing the cello and singing
and carried out research on the rites that sons must
perform for their father in Hindu mythology
she said her name was Tamil
that she was descended from that name that prowled through her blood
but that even if the name were false
it was nonetheless hers since it was the one by which
she wanted to be known and that she asked me
to write the dedication to the aforementioned Tamil woman
without lying truths because writers lie
and doctors also conceal the truth
that was true
and would I be so kind as to also respect the spelling of her name
which was she said of the utmost importance
in case of a mistake the aforesaid dedication would
no longer be to her but to someone else
like one of those many other women to whom I had assuredly
dedicated books recently
doubtlessly fervent admirers
but she didn't want to appear she said in the theory of unknown women
and would be angry with me if I couldn't understand why

she said that I shouldn't question her about anything
either about her past or her reasons for being in French Guiana
or about her emotional life but that after arriving
she'd become the mistress of a certain consul
whose vice-consul passed himself off as a creole octoroon
of Romanian descent a poet and man of letters
a sort of penniless Byzantine aristocrat who continually lamented
the golden-oiled skin of the prostitutes of Surinam
the former Dutch Guyana
who in his crepuscular verse
inspired by Ezra Pound announced he was *ready*
to make the night liquid
by cheating in every possible way with the blackest ass around
and whose beautiful blonde wife Ulrike
was from East Germany

she said that in Paris she'd lived in an apartment
on the Avenue Maréchal-de-Lattre-de-Tassigny
that she'd shared with an older man
an academic whose publications she'd proofread
for several years but who was the most despicable person
on the face of the earth because during all that time
he'd made love to her dishonestly to destroy and dominate her
without ever caressing her or talking about having a child
and the memory of it kept coming back
sometimes filling her with remorse and giving her a feeling
of vertigo whenever she remembered that diabolical
callous cruel soul who preferred to be left alone to write
getting up from bed completely naked to go back to his study
without saying a word
and yet she was sure she was the only woman
he'd ever loved

that relationship she said was all over now
but her regrets about having slept around so much
since she'd gone to bed with his closest friends
and cheated on him in front of everyone
came back to haunt her every night
but she understood her affairs
as being a sort of revenge in kind
she said that wasn't the main reason
for moving to South America
which might seem like exiling the victim
of a love affair that had lasted four years and seven months
during which she had abandoned her music
to be with this squalid man she had deceived
with so many lovers
and these infidelities that never ceased tormenting her
because she herself remained
unfaithful in act as well as thought
still surged up today like a secret vice
a ceaseless craving for men's eyes

especially for the melancholy in men's eyes
and these dark zones within herself
this secret vice that threw her off balance
were things she tried as hard as she could to conceal
something she evidently mistakenly feared since I didn't try
to find any flaws in her to take advantage of
she said that I could conjure up her heartache
her disappointed love as reasons for her exile
and I could even because I was a writer
that is a compulsive taleteller imagine she was condemned
to the jungle penal colony because of unrequited love
and disgust with men for whom
the basis of a relationship is to be as meagre
with their body as with their language
since she couldn't justify anything

she said I had the right to believe
that suddenly pulling out of the sexual embrace
of the lovers' embrace
was the reason why she was in French Guiana
but that in fact she had no idea what she'd put in those wandering letters
she had written me other than that she suffered
incomparably more from the way she had written them
because she said even though she hadn't known it
right from the beginning of that lovers' silence
she had been deeply affected by the breakup
incriminating the vice which she thought she'd left behind
when she'd failed so resoundingly
except in asking for the dedication that would help her to know
to understand the pain like the bite of pepper in a wound

since the taboo on words required me
never to tell anyone the secret of her life
although she suspected writers had
a dangerous propensity to use the lives of others
and even their own lives as material for their works
she said that even though she had the most absolute admiration
for the work of writers who mixed thought life fiction
knowledge as if they were all part of a single body
she felt reassured about it because I would refrain
from and resist the temptation to exploit her trivial existence
but that in any case as a physician
I would remain loyal to my inalienable oath
never to divulge the recesses of the souls
who confided in me

she said that this situation was unbearable
because on one hand I could choose
the mythical writer and taleteller while on the other
I suffered the same torments as Rabelais and Céline
so that I couldn't pretend to synthesize
literature and medicine by remaining immersed
in the suffering of others
and that now that she thought about it the dedication would give me
the chance to get rid of a few illusions
such as my humanist beliefs
because I had to choose the coda with which to tie up
the piece I was writing
now that it was too late in a way
to retreat because my soul had been confused by her presence
by the stroke of fortune as powerful as a cyclone
and that love was not decipherable
but that as a portraitist I should be able
at a glance
to write without being too obvious everything she inspired in me
because a person's entirety can only be grasped
through the eyes

she also said that nothing more would be given
on the thousandth night than on the first
and that despite her request
which she realized was ambiguous
and due to the fact that she'd been caught in her own game
I would spare her any personal questions
things as inconsequential as her age her race
the number of lovers she'd had
and that I would remain faithful to the secret I knew nothing about
to her past that was the inexhaustible source of her request
because to get back to my ability to read the light
emanating from others she said that I had
a gift for literature only my vocation had made me
a doctor because I heard the exasperated voice
buried within the bodies of others
indivisible from what carries it off
engulfed in the suffering it springs from
that was the meaning of the word vocation
the body of the Other calls out

she said that for these reasons I couldn't envisage
avoiding her request and that when I'd taken
the risk of studying medicine
and had torn myself away from literature which I loved so much
out of a guilty conscience
my own shabby fear of solitude and mediocre dread of art
from then on
I'd known that it would be ever more difficult
and complicated to renounce writing
since no one renounces a work of art
and in the end I shouldn't hesitate
to overcome one of the greatest of all follies
that of writing and healing that unimaginable one of speaking the body
at the risk of being packed off to the insane asylum
that of writing everything she inspired in me
the ideal situation since I didn't know a thing about her

I shouldn't hesitate she said to use
everything that medicine had shown me about the body
the voice that echoes within it
the silent soul of the body
of her own body since in the most mundane way
I was at her mercy but that way
she could provide me with stronger joys than thought and reflection
to answer her request calmly and above all straightforwardly
because grandiloquence kills emotion
though she had been moved by the background music
on the web site
and had concluded that I liked Baroque music
because she'd recognized with a sense of great happiness
the extract *Air pour les sauvages* from Rameau's opera-ballet
Les Indes galantes

she added that she preferred
to hear the piece played by an eighteenth-century orchestra
the only one that really knew how to play this monstrous music
with earthquakes surging out of narcotic perfumes
that all the other versions of the opera were kitsch
making it superficial and unbearable with their teasing
stock exoticism when the work had been written
without the help of either sorcerers or gods and that
in his vision of tragedy in colonial times
Rameau made the black warrior Adario's love
for the Indian princess Zima emerge triumphant
though she was courted by two white officers
whose attentions she rejected

and she said that she herself had played
the role of the Indian woman
at the conservatory and
that she didn't believe in that kind of coincidence
that if I had deliberately chosen
to use the masterpiece by the great Baroque composer
it was with the aim of providing subtle clues
about my writing because the titles of my books
Opéra, Tribu, Savanes, Théories Caraïbes
implicitly referred
to the force of the Baroque in the colonies
to the origin of musical theory to the music of Rameau
inspired by the dances of tribes in Louisiana
to the air for savages
a festival of the spirit and the senses that she listened to attentively
with the greatest nostalgia

she said that at the same time she wasn't duped by this *artifice*
because she wasn't an utter idiot
and that despite the erudite manoeuvre
in the form of a perfectly lucid musical quotation
perfectly clear to her mind brought up on classical rationalism
she said that I was unfortunately the real savage in the sense that
she said
opening up the senses is already a thought she said
that her proof was so convincing that I couldn't deny
her irrefutable arguments
her meticulous interpretation of the facts and accomplished logic
that for the reasons she had just put forward
she had discovered that I
the so-called doctor the so-called poet
was a savage a true savage
who only wanted to resurrect the agora of times long past
where philosophy art and science once conversed
and that there was every reason not to take me for the centre of the
universe
since to honour the secret savagery
that haunted her here in the Amazon she had just as savagely formulated
her request for a dedication
without squandering the secret *fold* of her presence

she also said it was against the dark backdrop
of the savages' melancholy that the Baroque continued to be
a challenge for European thought and art
the folds in the soul and recesses of matter
and that if I admired Rameau so much
it was because of the complexity of this learned and artistic character
obsessed by tradition musical theory
and his own instincts as a creator
haunted by the failure of reason and communication
revising his texts to please his audience
sometimes even sacrificing his most original ideas
when he was subjected
due to his creative daring
to the furious attacks of his contemporaries
who called him a *monster*

as to her own solitary presence
on the shore of the Maroni River she lived she said
without working at her true profession which was teaching the cello
she said Cayenne was a maritime expression that came into use
in the fourteenth century and meant
the barracks used by sailors while waiting for a destination
and that she hadn't for a moment dreamed of telling me about it
because ever since her arrival in the city she'd been intoxicated
by the charm of faraway voyages
and that young as she was and ready for any sacrifice
she wanted to gather all the world's multicoloured diversity
into her senses
and she remembered how when she arrived here a few months earlier
she'd thought she'd found
a haven as she waited to continue on to her own destination
in unknown lands
but that she didn't know anything about the city's colonial history
how it had been captured by the Dutch and then retaken
the fate of the Îles du Salut converted into penal colonies

she said that in order to understand such a lovely
painful history I shouldn't rely on reading
because a people's culture doesn't just come from books
but I should look at the way the shadows of the trees
lengthened over the Places des Palmistes at sunset
if they let me out of there before nightfall
even if the most important thing at the moment
because she didn't want to distort my impressions
was the quiver that she thought she'd felt
when she'd asked me to dedicate the book to her
as it was the first time she'd seen me in person she'd smelled
the sweet violence of vetiver on my skin

she said she'd struggled to compare the photograph
with her vision of the way I looked
as I so offhandedly
signed the books held out to me by the headless crowd
who were utterly unaware of her suffering
of her desire to find the image she remembered
she said that in that photograph
my spirit was filled with the images of childhood
of market words and headscarves
of girls who urinated spreading their legs
and the urine mixed with the scent of almonds
she said that childhood was an admirable time of healthy warmth
and that as soon as classes were over
my mother would leave me with the maids
in a country house
that was a paradise of women
the maids were mulattos and smelled of vetiver
and not a trace of their mango-coloured faces remained
in the family photo albums

she said my childhood countryside was haunted
by the sound of hissing steam boilers
and the trumpeting of stills as the vapours climbed
because my uncles built a factory for distilling essential oils
and that I remembered a reddish liquid
that flowed out of the piping and turned the river to blood
that the house river vetiver factory seemed to me
now and forever the centre of the world
and that in this paradise where I'd known the anguish of separation
I had grown up amid the liveliness of machines
and said farewell to the silence of roots
because my childhood had also been filled
with longed-for cyclones

when she saw me she said she stared at the reconstructed image
to try to find an attitude at once familiar and enigmatic
because I wore the same style of clothing
despite the years that had gone by
the twill suit
and same bow tie that I knotted with liberated nonchalance
and in many ways I was even more nostalgic
than I liked to admit because nothing
not even my way of looking at the Caribbean colonies had changed
though my picture had become her thing
her spiritual thing
she was afraid people around me
would try to make off with my image
and tire me out by wearing down my nerves
while she had never ceased to harp on tirelessly
about her request since she didn't feel that
she'd settled the question of our origins

she said that the more she repeated her request
the more she felt in the rhythm of my own blood
an infinitely sweet and inexorable
total loss had been removed from me
a kind of hemorrhage of the sky disgorging its waters
a weakness of the body that vitiated my consciousness
and that she needed to have my image at any cost
because she was afraid of invisible things
and that I should know that as a writer
and a doctor that each person's suffering
always seems greatest
and that what gave her the energy to go on
was the sound of water flowing from one stone to another
and that apart from the quivering in a hidden zone
my appearance hadn't excited her
and that she'd noticed my long hands
which had made her think not of music
coming from those fingers
music that would allow her to scratch at my face
and eyes so she could get behind me
but of the supple gestures associated with writing a dedication

she said that she'd once been rather beautiful
but that the slight fading of her beauty
in no way discredited her request
or diminished what it
presupposed in terms of the loss of beauty and
seeing as I had never set eyes on her before
I didn't have any points of comparison
beyond the other women in the crowd
unless I went back into her past
being so independent by nature
but that she counted on my bourgeois education
to spare her the affront of anamnesis
though because I was a physician she was ready to reveal
the vague malaise she'd been suffering from lately
without being able to do much about it
as if she'd been caught up in a nocturnal spiral
unable to speak her mother tongue
which became phantasmal almost empty in her mouth
and that she no longer worried about trying to identify
the blurred image in her memory
that the malaise came from

she said that she had been soothed by the soft intonations
of men's voices that had brought her out of this waking coma
which cast a murky light on her appetite
for men and that every day
she would spend long hours lingering over the tables
strewn with books until they announced that the book fair
was closing but that she never bothered anyone
because every day she felt more assured
and would stroll among aisles with a newfound ease
she said that she would enter the fair in mid-afternoon
and wouldn't leave till the sun had set
and darkness returned
and that she was vaguely aware of the inappropriateness
of her conduct but that she herself couldn't
judge because every day her turmoil grew

she said that right off she'd craved
the smell of vetiver on my skin
she'd noticed she said that I'd lowered my eyes
when I'd entered the hotel room
and found her nude helpless
crouched on the bed and that had touched her
because she'd always thought that poets didn't have any inner life
they had nothing but modesty and that she'd especially appreciated
despite the unusual nature of her presence
in my hotel room and especially undressed in my bed
that I had the decency not to ask her
why or how she had gotten in and what
she was doing there because she was an honest woman
and her nudity could be a sign of love
an enduring love and that all love is enduring
even when we know it is short-lived
and that a love that ends was never love

the questions with simple answers
that she preferred not to ask she said
would aggravate her embarrassment since she found herself
obliged to betray the contacts
she'd benefitted from by being the consul's mistress
she said that I didn't ask her anything
and that I pretended not to remember
the book I'd supposedly dedicated to her after the first few minutes
during which the look on my face
didn't show the least surprise and that I didn't speak
a word
but simply sat at the foot of the bed at an angle to
her
without looking her over and that when she turned on
the television which several times a day and even at night
replayed the program about me
in which I strolled through the streets of Cayenne
talking about Les Cayes my birthplace
vestiges of the past the Lucayo Indians
I was descended from and whom I'd thus never forgotten
the program which I still hadn't seen
because she said I refused to watch myself on television

she said that the cathode-ray screen
after an abrupt burst of intensity
had suddenly gone blank
plunging the room into darkness
and then sparks had shot out
while an acrid smoke filled the room
she said that the manuscript piled up on
top of the television set had caught fire
like very old books on the highest shelves
and that it told the story of the calabash filled with golden jewels
the night by the light of a candle going up the Maroni River
like the great birds that sleep beneath the earth
that it was the manuscript of the *magically realistic* stories
of the consul general whose *ghostwriter* she'd been
just as long ago in Paris
when she'd corrected her lover's articles

she said she loved murmuring my name
in the silence at last perceptible in the room
and that before entering my room she had stopped
in front of a map of the world and had pressed her face
against two cities
suddenly measuring the vastness of latitudes
the beauty of the tropics dreamed like this made her close her eyes
and at that moment of supreme closeness
she dreamed a naked woman stretched out
across the warmth of the Equator
and that our shadows collided
without destroying the night
there where male mixes with female
in a fragrant and desperate predation
in the intense dread that spreads out
when they fall silent shivering on the shores of rivers
in hotel rooms that are also shores
in beds that are riverbanks
their nakedness covered by the green waters of vetiver

IV

Basse-Terre

above or below the wind
it rushes at the coast there where the grass grazes
linear glabrous leaves obscene along the edges
a great thanks
for the calming decoctions against asthma fever
migraines and other introsusceptions
roots readers of entrails sticky with tenesmus
or for the coils of points that subside
a great thanks devotedly as you pray
for the rhizomes of earth that drip
to the breath of monsoons
you are even more chaste lying among the stubble
your ankle swollen with edema
blood turning blue around the malleolus and your large lips
filled with juice
teeming at the edge
the one who described them had never seen any as dark
groves the colour of burnt earth drawn from the brain
night has come to bow
tenderly to help us give up our melancholy
the essence of vetiver dripping down your thighs once again

the weary look hopes to immortalize the setting
in a photograph
the sleeping veranda in the day that's never day
there's a strangeness in your eyelids closed once again
sin and may
the heart's collapse in the midst of lovers
swallow the stars that your gaze follows
as the mating couples reach rapture
the stars can't draw any nearer
despite the caresses spurting from sex
they crack and die in the fields of the dead
like the children of aborted women
and may they return to life in your womb

the moaning of the mulatto woman is life
delaying what awaits me in hell
in Santiago she walked upon the coffee-coloured
wooden floor
the trees bearing women
were seized by an epilepsy of glory
right in my mouth
having drunk the milk of the manchineel tree
but at the foot of the most beautiful one
came the slow tread of crabs
carrying off her dress across the darkening sand
beneath the open sky I search for the places
the south puts an end
to the winter light

I don't dare say what takes me to the Indies
East and West reverse in their waters
I walk on the sand
as if in a cloister
the arches of light out of line in the garden
beyond which nothing stirs
save the whips of latania beneath the rain
the spume at the corners of their lips when the lovers
scan what bloodless remains are left under their pleura
or else the fray of dogs upon the shore
blind they do not hear our cries

there's a wheezing of wind along the paths
suggesting invisible presences
except that the eye's jolts betray
the sight of memorable rock slides
that smash against the slopes
after at last having left the ferocious towns and countries
far from the cities where people delight in a stupor
of alcohol and garish melodies
among the gathered signs of exodus
taking pictures of the naked lover and the stigmata of the cangue
around her neck
in the merciless light for open graves
years ago they would bury her alive
here's the lover's head here's the clay of eyes eyes

we're lucky to be able to flee
the pointless poignant winter even for
a few days
in the south where the crumbling light
is warm upon the skin
melanin as brazen as it is greedy
we believed then in God in the reddening of a star
infinitely dying
wife of three races leading the black rabble like cattle
to the great provinces of salt
the thin multitudes wandering across the earth
they want to touch you with their hands
the fever sheets see your pubis once again
and slip in the reed pen

I swear on my family's misfortune
that I lost the Book of my father's father
I hesitate to damn them all except for Brennus
what a name Latin again
the fair-skinned uncle on his gelded beast defying
the American occupiers
when the mulatto woman woke me from my sleep
calling me an abortionist who fed at her breasts
swollen with eternal milk the nubile left one
was licked by flames
it was then that a pile of flesh flowed out between her legs
beneath the shower nine months before the mysterious
birth
alerted by a ray of light coming from the shower stall
I saw
the little blood-streaked thing
in its cradle of chorion
lying lying
at the edge of the sink

all the leaves of paper bound together upon which
I am dying
herbs hidden from others
can't uproot the hope of birth
this evening I'll go to the maternity ward
and take the child who recognizes my voice
from your womb
between your smooth thighs still touched by the salt of the first
sea
when the time comes to choose a name
for his jade eyes that are the gift of God
we will chant that of the ancestor

in honour of John Keats spare him the galloping tuberculosis
William Carlos Williams the obstetrician crossing out poems
on the back of prescriptions
without forgetting Friedrich Schiller
rereading you today and Gottfried Benn
survived a moment of dribble in the navel of whiteness
Leena in Antwerp in carnal charity
kiss as I do kissing her human feet
you
all attract my trembling homages
doctors poets praying to Apollo the Sun God without whom
everything would be less
the books the hymns crying out love
on behalf of humans

may it please the living
Lorand Gaspar my double from the Balkans
how much shrapnel have you extracted from our guts
your hands buried in the Judean dust
or else Jean Métellus with his Mandingo profile
at dawn you colloquialize the duty of exile
but there is no more exile
there is
the trace now almost effaced of the ancient crime
the most beautiful words since the gospels covered with asthma
the creole eloquence moves off down the hospital corridors
as the procession of ageing Westerners goes by
may it please those who watch over you at night
to lead poetry out of the poem
return it to the words of the people
poetry
grafted to those who bleed like saints

poor little head emerged living from your reign
so that my arms can hug it
O the brightness of his child's face on my madness
crying
we were both forceful and pure
when at the Plantation
the dancer love inspired us with the music of love
and on the esplanade
the guard's ignorant face as he made his rounds
stiffened to attention
as if possessed by prosaic demons
and the walls
suddenly aflame
scattered the deepest moans to our ears
and the Sainte-Soufrière volcano was getting ready to erupt
as the lava emanated down the slopes
patient imminent very black

in the mass of basalt organs
I looked for the places of oblivion
not the slightest soul nor the slightest book
aside from those that conserved
the voices of women
no longer knowing who or what was guiding me
or even if the agony was mine
of kids disguised as bulls
who cracked their whips across the asphalt with a sinister hand
before they'd gone on to crime
held out their long pleading hands
to the tourist woman with white breasts
the sweat beaded on her sleeping skin
while the pious crowds
took leaf baths
under rain water
the remnants of the era went off to Lent
with armfuls of rock salt and ammonia

I wandered through the city
carried along by a kind of old joy
or narrative force
in search of the shadow of the arcades a young man
with blue skin also roamed about with the air of a sorcerer
an abandoned slave
sad body twisted with hunger
his hands and feet as red as annatto
asked me for work so he could reclaim his dignity
a bit of starch mutely for his guts
suddenly enraged and raving insanely
the prince of Angola or Ghana was leaving to fight in the alleyways
that hum with unreal things
awouah awouah
may the saint's son find salvation here
in the high nakedness of poetry

condition of derelict blacks held for over two months
in the Basse-Terre jail who
if still unclaimed by July 31 of this month
will be sold at the behest of the Honourable Public Prosecutor
and in the presence of the Distinguished Central Administrative
Commissioner
Julien rebellious around 35 years of age claiming to be free
afterward belonged to one Rémy a freeman
his maternal grandfather having died in jail
in Basse-Terre on August 16 1810
Louis a negro from the coast of Guinea
says he is a freeman from Puerto Rico
without a scrap of paper to prove his identity
in jail on April 7 1811
Angèle a creole negress about 27 years old
claiming to belong to the widow Madame Mauperthuis du Moule and
unknown to that woman as being her property
in jail on April 25 1811

outside the rooms the sentence to being whipped
by the public authorities is carried out
at the four corners of the cities and towns
so she'll be known by everyone
on the main street corners
at junctions and the usual places
sentenced to shackles
she wears an iron collar set with long spikes
is executed in the central square of Basse-Terre
on this very spot that in the nineteenth century
was known as the Bridge Herb Market

condition of runaway slaves held at the Basse-Terre jail
on September 15 1815
a new negro of the Ibo nation
about 22 years of age unable to give his name
or that of his master
dressed in pants and a coarse cotton shirt
Joseph a young negro who calls himself Saint-Cloud
of Petit-Bourg
Marie-Thérèse belonging to Monsieur Brescon
Adélaïde a negress belonging to Monsieur Pincevoir
du Lamentin

this is where they used to announce important news
to the sound of a tambourine
besides the sentence to being clapped in irons reserved for slaves
they publicly displayed free persons of colour
who had committed misdeeds
the penalty of being shackled in public included
wearing a sign around your neck
on which they wrote the nature of your crime
in 1822 the slave Jérémie property of Sieur Casamayor
a merchant in Basse-Terre was condemned
to two hours in irons wearing a sign
that read
slave who struck a white
and to three years in the galleys

the beauty of the architecture took its place
in the saffron light
a somewhat heavy euphoria swept over the city
the courthouse threw its last steps
into the rising tide
of the serous sea
behind the modern style of the white
façades
but Ali Tur's poetry is still there
I searched the cloistered galleries
the courts are in session for sordid affairs of rape
and debauchery
what then is the lack of virtue
two guys from Dominica get sentenced to hard time
for smuggling Haitians
their boats are seized and the illegals
sent back to their ferocious homeland
they're like Charrons of the tombstone sea

the evening is pure
warmongers have spray-painted
Stars of David on the basilica
of the Virgin Mary
dogs bark at candles that sputter
the gestures of someone pissing on the allamandas
solitude of the black beggar in his rags
staggering
his death will be white with the January rains
a tall slender girl running after the dogs
she laughed in the hedges
and her long legs landed on the islands like aircraft carriers
afraid of being run over by her happiness at being alive
I left the city for the pepper-covered hills
and black waters
alive with moray eels and catfish
my life offered up to the people of women

the day died away and the city on the open sea
people filled the streets
pressed tightly against the black air of the streets
lined with splinters
verandas wooden lacework
gables
and I saw what I was supposed to see
another carnival Sunday
people of colour
people of my race
let no one dream of it let no one dream
of deserting the people of his race
guys spitting out obscenities
sweating under the great drum
I'd rather mix together the skins of people and beasts
the smell of vetiver in the crowded streets
it's at the crossroads that they burn the roots
in a kind of incense-burner
but the new wives in their bright dresses
looked around for deflowered places

it was hard to leave the boundaries
for the waters of Grande-Rivière
where the fires glided along
a desire for a pilgrimage to the coffee slopes
the horrible slave huts sagging relics
open to the stridence
why after so many modern centuries
travel along the road of snares and passes
continually opening chasms
see the undressed canna plants slumbering almond trees
the pagan elation of tree trunks surges forward
haunted by epiphytes
to take the half-breed Asian among the stubble
animal style
the shade of the trees like a sheet
thus fulfilling the highest marriage
old hydraulic machines obsess me
flat boxes spread with green coffee that you'd cover over
making the gestures of someone searching among
the planks for the collar of servitude
the mallets of the guayacum trees thirsty for framing
O prowler

the vetiver people have kept watch through the night
over the birth of a new myth
dawn is terrible for the madman
who believed in the holy book
how melancholy is the sky in Tamil Nadu
after your exile on the Peruvian sea
the Antillean couch grass shines
against the sides of temples
the people have descended in the dust
and the washed-out saris
are stained with dung
the movie screens show your past
the fear in your eyes so long
and your eyes no longer believe in this grandiose century
I give you a few tears
for the herb that was brought from the Orient
dark black priestesses heavy with science
Satyavati Gandhakali
lovers the colour of charity of copper
will throw Dravidian perfumes upon my ashes